This book belongs to:

Please sign here:_____

and here:_____

and here:_____

Ellie

the
Tooting Elf

By
Humor Heals Us

Ellie would be what you call a loner elf. It wasn't that she didn't like having friends. She just didn't know how to make them. And it didn't help that she was extremely shy.

Ellie sat at her desk most days dreaming up the next big toy for children all around the world.

It seemed as though everyone had a talent, except Ellie.

Then there was Carol the elf. She could carve the most beautiful wooden toys imaginable.

The strongest elf was Miles. When he and his brother, Kilometers, weren't working out, you could find him putting his muscles to use.

One day while she was in the lab, she came upon an idea for some colorful blocks.

At the toy presentation later that week, Ellie felt her tummy swirling and it took all of her to keep her toots in. Mostly, anyways.

Santa instantly fell in love with it. He thought of so many kids that might like this new creation so he ordered a bunch of them to be made. One billion to be exact!

Ellie was so happy! All the other elves came rushing over to give her high-fives and congratulate her.

That Christmas many kids put legos on their list.
And Ellie went back to her lab to work on more toy ideas.

Follow us on FB and IG @humorhealsus
To vote on new title names and freebies,
visit us at humorhealsus.com for more
information.

 @humorhealsus

 @humorhealsus